ALL I GOT
IS WHAT I FEEL
INSIDE LOOKING AT
YOUR OUTSIDE

MATHEW (MATT) PHILLIPS

authorHOUSE®

AuthorHouse™
1663 Liberty Drive
Bloomington, IN 47403
www.authorhouse.com
Phone: 1 (800) 839-8640

Published by AuthorHouse 02/08/2019

ISBN: 978-1-5462-7982-2 (sc)
ISBN: 978-1-5462-7981-5 (e)

Print information available on the last page.

This book is printed on acid-free paper.

External Surfaces are all we have of each other. Another person's experiences may or may not be in line with ours. We can never know for sure.

We can never be inside each other's skin to know for sure what another feels like. External feeling and observations are all we've ever had of one another. "All I got is what I feel inside looking at other peoples outside"... is what I got to remember.

Since the greatest challenge in life is living it while acknowledging its lack of predictability, the closest we can come is having a "miniature" goal in each step we take. A goal is if we can get healthy enough to live in the next moment and then healthy enough to live in the next moment and each moment after do the same way that would be worth putting in writing and putting in our pocket to carry with us "to read frequently." No matter what our goal is, the first step is always the "physical step" we take with our feet.

A true leader polishes their podium "independent" of "titles" or "labels" they may be given.

Instead of depending on a "leader" to give you "ideas", think about this for a second. Just you and another person walking along and discussing ideas telling yourself "an idea" is only the best idea until a better idea comes along?

Something for People
everywhere to keep in
mind as a reason for
'Peace' is the simple fact
that the awareness that it
is easier to determine the
'accuracy' of something
closer compared to
when something that
is happening off in a
distance.

If another person has a pain in one of their feet when they are saying something to us, that effects the mood and thereby what they are saying; we may never know this when listening to them. In realizing this,

we can never know what
another person feels like
because we can never feel
the way another feels
other than what external
observations tell us about
each other.

If Mankind can run the 4-minute mile, it could feed everyone on earth.

THINK ABOUT THIS: Success is just generating positive things around your body and its just spreading in an outward direction from there.

When I finally get to Heaven, I visualize my telling Jesus; I'll take my coffee black!

People are like teabags.
We don't know our inner
strength until we are put
into hot water.

Everything begins with an idea. We know 100% our chances of success if we don't try.

Judging another human being is equivalent to assuming you are that person, substituting your experiences in life for his or hers.

Something for People everywhere to keep in mind as a reason for 'Peace' is the simple fact that the awareness that it is easier to determine the 'accuracy' of something closer compared to when something that is happening off in a distance.

Even if you do influence things at a distance from your body, a brilliant question is to ask what you are able to accomplish right outside your "skin?"

Th external packaging of people, such as dress and grooming, is something that a person has taken to take care of his or herself.

We should remember the best we can do is create favorable conditions, based on a proven track record on an ongoing basis in so many, if not most instances.

Another reason we need to realize we c an never know what another is feeling
is that we all are each forever changing.

Regardless of what a person has done in the past, their future is 'unblemished.' They have a 'clean slate.' A society that fails to recognize this, point it out regularly and make it a "Very Big Part of what's going on when judging others" is a "less than intelligent society."

If we could or it was possible to know what a person is feeling, just for a second, they would change the next second as we are forever changing beings internally and externally. All we have is the external observation of each other.

You can't turn 'nothing' into 'something.' But there is 'Wisdom' in coming as 'close as possible!'

What my message intends
to clearly point out is it
is "The point where the
sound of the human voices
with the best ideas get
transferred to "physical
reality

It's the transfer of where the greatest ideas of what is said with people's voices to making things become 'physical reality' that is important.

It's not just the 'voices' of people with "good ideas," but delivery of the "End product" that 'they are talking about

Wisdom to carry once we get out of school "It's not just what I know, but what I will come to know that is important."

We don't know what another person is going to say until they talk... that's why they are talking.

Think about this for yourself: Movies, books, songs and speeches that get well known everywhere are just "successfully" promoted 'messages' and words like "Fame" are attached to them.

Is this an "obvious, but good question": How much does the average person, when setting in a room, know about what's going on in the World? Factor in the "idea" that since the greatest challenge in life is living it while acknowledging it's lack of predictability, the closest we can do is have a "miniature goal" in each step we take

A person who is doing something Really Great may sense they are going to be around a while, but does have to get along with the "idea of dying."

No matter what anyone does on Earth, we need to study what happened to them on "their corner of the Earth" to get them to do what they have done.

As an example, I have to realize if I should ever find myself standing before the creator of the Universe, (God if you will), all I have is God's external image. I will not even know what God is thinking until I see this great power's lips move. This analogy has been a great reward as well as a comfort for me as I hope it will for all, who might read these "words".

People accomplish things
on a local level, then they
are promoted. Think
about what happens,
if we, humanity, fail to
recognize this.

How can you make your immediate environment compliment your life? You will take your first step there!

Suppose you visualize communication with other people like a two lane highway, you're sending information to them down one lane and their sending information to you back down the other. With this in mind, it should be fine with your leaders, the two lane highway you have with them as human beings, they tell you how they determine when it comes to their governing, how they stop sending information to you down their lane while they are deciding with other leaders what to do. Regarding the saying "As people, we don't believe what we see, but see what we believe.", what helps us understand it better is when you think about the fact that the closer you get to something, details become more clear.

Really, the Earth is part of the foundation beneath our "houses."

The only way any of us get along, in any relationship, is by creating favorable conditions around each other.

The greatest quality a leader can have is a "very clear memory" of what it is like to be a follower.

There is no greater
satisfaction than setting
something before
someone's eyes to get
a point across finding
it "unnecessary" to say
words from a person's
mouth!

Humanity making the transition from trying to make their points with words from the mouths of people to making their points by setting ideas that have been completed before people's eyes is just "education."

If the discussion of "fear" comes up, mention of the factor that when one gets closer to something, details become more clear.

When you plan something, ask yourself how important is looking at the details of the 1st step and then when taking the first step plan the details of the very next step and then doing the very same thing each step thereafter until the goal is accomplished? It should be pointed out that since the greatest challenge

in life is living it while
acknowledging it's lack of
predictability coming as
close as possible having a
"miniature goal" in each
step is really all that one
can do.

Politicians are trying to
get things done with their
mouths and things need
to be done with hands.

If any of us plan to accomplish anything, if we have not planned the details of the 1st step, we are not ready.

Is there wisdom in the idea of people talking less and simply exploring things we can do to improve things on the planet?

Words said from the mouth have no guarantee where they are going to land compared to written words which, obviously, have already landed." It is people becoming aware of this that is causing leaders to become less effective with words that are spoken from their mouth.

THERE IS SO MUCH GOOD IN THE WORST OF US AND BAD IN THE BEST OF US THAT IT IL-BEHOOVES ANY OF US TO CRITICIZE THE REST OF US

WHEN THE SAYING "There is so much good in the worst of us and bad in the best of us." is forgot are people getting off track? DO YOU HAVE TO BE IN A CERTAIN COUNTRY FOR THIS TO MAKE SENSE?

It's intelligent actions of the masses that leaders react to. Things that get done are based on who does the best convincing. All we do is convince each other as people. It doesn't matter who you are. Lay your ideas before the eyes of others and let that do you're talking if you can. We should never forget, people made the laws, people can change the laws.

In the context of "Eternity," our age means nothing on this earth.

To say there is a Hell that God is going to through people into is to say God is giving up on something. I don't believe God gives up on anything!

People who govern from a distance should be more than happy to explain how they do it since the further away you are from something details are less clear.

Printed in the United States
By Bookmasters